Unlocking the
Wealth
NABAL KISHORE PANDE

1

Preface

In the rapidly evolving landscape of the digital era, a resounding buzz has been generated by the emergence of non-fungible tokens, or NFTs, a groundbreaking manifestation of the potential of blockchain technology. This intriguing innovation has captured the collective imagination of individuals across the globe, embodying a fusion of both the digital and financial realms. With their unique ability to represent ownership of digital assets, NFTs have swiftly risen to prominence, serving as a dynamic symbol of the ongoing metamorphosis in the way we perceive and interact with wealth and ownership.

NFTs, in their essence, are veritable digital certificates of authenticity, granting owners exclusive rights to a specific digital asset, whether it be a piece of art, a collectable, or a virtual real estate property, among various other possibilities. This revolutionary concept has opened up a realm of unprecedented opportunities for creators and collectors alike, empowering them to establish a new paradigm in the economy of digital assets. By leveraging the underlying technology of blockchain, NFTs have introduced a secure and transparent method of ownership, revolutionizing the way we perceive and engage with the concept of value in the digital domain.

The allure of NFTs lies not only in their capacity to democratize the ownership of digital assets but also in their inherent potential to unlock previously untapped avenues of wealth creation. With the advent of NFTs, the traditional barriers to entry into the world of art, entertainment, and even real estate have been dismantled, enabling a wider and more diverse array of individuals to participate in and benefit from the burgeoning digital economy. This democratization has infused a sense of empowerment among creators, who now have the means to directly monetize their digital creations, thus challenging the conventional structures of the art and entertainment industries.

Moreover, the exponential growth of the NFT market has catalyzed a surge in investment opportunities, fostering a dynamic ecosystem that entices both seasoned investors and newcomers alike. The sheer diversity of digital assets that can be tokenized as NFTs, ranging from digital art and music to virtual real estate and even tweets, has broadened the scope of investment portfolios, introducing a new asset class with immense potential for value appreciation. As a result, the realm of NFTs has become a fertile ground for financial innovation, where individuals can strategically position themselves to harness the rewards of this burgeoning digital economy.

Amidst the exuberance surrounding the potential wealth creation opportunities facilitated by NFTs, it is imperative to recognize the transformative potential of this technology beyond its financial implications. NFTs have paved the way for a paradigm shift in the way we perceive and interact with digital ownership, fostering a new sense of digital identity and belonging within virtual communities. This sense of belonging has not only fostered vibrant online communities centred around shared interests but has also catalyzed the development of new digital ecosystems, fostering collaboration, and innovation on an unprecedented scale.

However, alongside the immense promise and potential that NFTs embody, it is essential to acknowledge the complex web of challenges and controversies that accompany this nascent technology. The surge in energy consumption and environmental concerns related to the mining and trading of NFTs has sparked debates about the sustainability and ethical implications of the NFT market. Moreover, issues related to copyright infringement and the proliferation of counterfeit NFTs have underscored the need for a robust regulatory framework to safeguard the interests of creators and investors.

Against this backdrop, our exploration of the power of wealth with NFTs seeks to provide a comprehensive understanding of the multifaceted dimensions of this transformative technology. By delving into the intricate interplay of technology, finance, art, and culture, this book aims to unravel the enigmatic allure of NFTs, offering readers a nuanced perspective on the transformative potential and the challenges that accompany this groundbreaking innovation. Through a meticulous examination of case studies, expert insights, and practical guidance, we aspire to equip our readers with the knowledge and tools necessary to navigate the complex terrain of NFTs and harness their potential for wealth creation in the digital age.

Acknowledgements

I owe a profound debt of gratitude to the exceptional minds who have illuminated the path to understanding the intricacies of Non-Fungible Tokens (NFTs) and their profound impact on the world of wealth creation. Their unwavering support and unparalleled expertise have been instrumental in the creation of this comprehensive exploration of the transformative power of NFTs.

First and foremost, I extend my heartfelt appreciation to the trailblazing pioneers in the blockchain industry, whose groundbreaking contributions have paved the way for the emergence of NFTs as a disruptive force in the digital economy. Their visionary insights and tireless dedication to technological innovation have set the stage for the widespread adoption of NFTs in various sectors, from art and entertainment to real estate and beyond.

I am indebted to the NFT experts whose deep understanding of the intricate mechanics of this groundbreaking technology has provided the necessary foundation for the in-depth analysis presented within these pages. Their willingness to share their knowledge and experiences has allowed us to unravel the complexities of NFT creation, ownership, and trading, providing readers with a comprehensive understanding of the vast potential inherent in this transformative digital asset.

Furthermore, I am profoundly grateful for the collaboration and input from the creative minds within the art world, whose visionary use of NFTs has redefined the very essence of artistic expression and ownership. Their innovative approaches to digital art and the integration of NFTs have not only revolutionized the art market but have also inspired a new generation of artists to explore the uncharted territory of digital ownership and distribution.

In the realm of finance, my heartfelt appreciation goes to the financial experts whose profound insights into the economic implications of NFTs have enriched the narrative presented in this book. Their comprehensive understanding of the financial implications of

NFT ownership, investment strategies, and market trends has provided readers with a nuanced perspective on the transformative potential of NFTs in the realm of wealth creation and investment.

The invaluable contributions of legal scholars and experts in the field of digital ownership have played an integral role in shaping the discussion surrounding the legal implications and challenges associated with NFTs. Their expertise in navigating the complex legal landscape of digital ownership and intellectual property rights has shed light on the legal considerations that must be taken into account when engaging with NFTs, ensuring that readers are equipped with the necessary knowledge to navigate this rapidly evolving digital landscape with confidence and security.

I am indebted to the environmental advocates and sustainability experts who have highlighted the environmental impact of NFTs and the importance of implementing sustainable practices within the NFT ecosystem. Their commitment to fostering environmentally conscious practices within the digital realm has underscored the necessity of adopting eco-friendly approaches to NFT creation and trading, ensuring that the transformative potential of NFTs is harnessed in a manner that is both ethically and environmentally responsible.

Additionally, I extend my sincere appreciation to the technological innovators and visionaries whose commitment to pushing the boundaries of technological advancement has catalyzed the continuous evolution of the NFT landscape. Their pioneering efforts in developing cutting-edge technologies and platforms have facilitated the seamless integration of NFTs into various industries, propelling the transformative power of NFTs to unprecedented heights and unlocking new realms of possibility within the digital economy.

I am grateful for the invaluable insights provided by the community builders and thought leaders who have fostered vibrant and inclusive communities within the NFT ecosystem. Their dedication to cultivating a collaborative and supportive environment for NFT enthusiasts, creators, and collectors has fostered a sense of belonging and camaraderie within the NFT community, facilitating the exchange of ideas and the cultivation of a shared vision for the future of NFTs and wealth creation.

Furthermore, I express my gratitude to the investors and entrepreneurs whose innovative approaches to NFT investment and entrepreneurship have exemplified the transformative potential of NFTs as a viable investment vehicle. Their entrepreneurial spirit and willingness to embrace risk have demonstrated the immense opportunities that exist within the NFT market, inspiring a new generation of investors to explore the potential of NFTs as a lucrative and dynamic asset class within their investment portfolios.

I am profoundly grateful for the unwavering support and encouragement from my peers and colleagues, whose constructive feedback and insightful perspectives have been instrumental in shaping the narrative of this book. Their unwavering support and encouragement have served as a constant source of inspiration, propelling me forward on this journey of exploration and discovery within the dynamic and ever-evolving landscape of NFTs and wealth creation.

To my family and friends, I extend my heartfelt gratitude for their unwavering support and encouragement throughout the writing process. Their unyielding belief in my abilities and their steadfast encouragement have provided me with the strength and determination to see this project through to fruition, underscoring the importance of having a strong support system during the pursuit of ambitious endeavours.

Last but certainly not least, I extend my deepest appreciation to the readers and enthusiasts who have embarked on this enlightening journey of exploration with me. Your unwavering curiosity and passion for learning have served as the driving force behind the creation of this book, inspiring me to delve deeper into the complexities of NFTs and their transformative potential within the realm of wealth creation. May this exploration serve as a guiding light on your journey of discovery within the captivating world of NFTs and the potent magic of wealth creation.

Prologue

In an age where technological marvels continuously redefine the boundaries of human innovation, Non-Fungible Tokens (NFTs) have emerged as the veritable flag-bearers of a new era. They represent a potent fusion of artistry, finance, and digital wizardry, igniting a transformative fire that has spread like wildfire across the global financial landscape. As we embark on this literary journey into the enchanting realm of NFTs, we are poised to uncover the multifaceted magic they wield in shaping the very essence of wealth creation and redefining the concept of value itself.

The genesis of NFTs can be traced back to the fertile grounds of blockchain technology, where the concepts of uniqueness, indivisibility, and cryptographic security converged to birth a revolutionary digital asset class. Unlike their fungible counterparts, NFTs, with their inherent uniqueness and indivisibility, have shattered the traditional confines of asset exchange, giving rise to an unprecedented era of creative expression and financial empowerment.

At their core, NFTs are not merely digital tokens; they are conduits of storytelling, windows into the souls of their creators, and vessels that carry the essence of both tangible and intangible art forms. Each NFT encapsulates a narrative, an emotion, or a piece of history, creating an intricate tapestry that intertwines technology with human expression, beckoning individuals to delve deeper into the very heart of what it means to be a creator and a collector in this digital age.

The allure of NFTs does not solely reside in their artistic appeal; it extends to the dynamic realms of entertainment, gaming, and the ever-expanding universe of virtual experiences. Through NFTs, musicians have found a new medium to forge intimate connections with their audiences, offering exclusive access to unreleased tracks or limited-edition memorabilia, thus revolutionizing how music is both consumed and cherished.

Moreover, the gaming industry, long revered for its ability to transport individuals into alternate realities, has undergone a metamorphosis with the integration of NFTs. Virtual assets within gaming ecosystems have acquired a newfound sense of permanence and value, allowing gamers to own, trade, and cherish in-game items as they would physical possessions, thereby fostering an unprecedented sense of ownership and engagement within virtual worlds.

Beyond the realms of art, entertainment, and gaming, NFTs have begun to leave their indelible mark on the landscape of real estate, offering a digital gateway to the world of property ownership and investment. The once laborious and convoluted processes of real estate transactions have now been streamlined and made more accessible through the implementation of NFTs, providing individuals with a transparent and efficient means of engaging with the ever-evolving global real estate market.

However, within this heady mix of innovation and opportunity, one cannot overlook the complexities and challenges that accompany the widespread adoption of NFTs. As these digital assets continue to gain traction, concerns surrounding their environmental impact, authenticity, and regulatory frameworks have come to the forefront, prompting a rigorous examination of the ethical and legal implications inherent in the NFT ecosystem.

Despite these challenges, the underlying potential of NFTs remains undeniably compelling, serving as a testament to the resilience and adaptability of human creativity and financial ingenuity. The journey that lies ahead within the pages of this book transcends the conventional confines of wealth and invites readers to partake in a transformative odyssey, where digital art, virtual experiences, and financial prosperity converge to redefine the very essence of wealth creation in the 21st century. So, embark with us on this riveting exploration of the potent magic of wealth with NFTs, and witness firsthand the unfolding of a new chapter in the annals of global finance and digital innovation.

The Birth of NFTs

In the captivating landscape of blockchain technology and digital innovation, a remarkable phenomenon known as Non-Fungible Tokens (NFTs) has emerged. These tokens, often referred to as the "digital certificates of authenticity," are the magical key to unlocking a new realm of wealth and creativity. As we embark on our journey through the fascinating world of NFTs, we must begin at the genesis – the birth of NFTs.

The Genesis of NFTs: NFTs, in essence, are a product of the intricate and ingenious world of blockchain technology. They first made their appearance in the early 2010s, a period when the concept of digital ownership was still taking baby steps. It was in 2012 when J.R. Willett's proposal for a concept called "coloured coins" laid the foundational idea for NFTs. However, it was not until 2017 that the term "Non-Fungible Token" was coined and embraced.

Fungibility vs. Non-Fungibility: Understanding the concept of NFTs requires a clear distinction between the terms "fungible" and "non-fungible." Fungible assets, like cryptocurrencies, are interchangeable with one another. For instance, one Bitcoin is equal in value to another Bitcoin. Non-fungible assets, on the other hand, are unique and irreplaceable. Each NFT possesses a distinct value, tied to its rarity, provenance, or utility.

Ethereum: The Pioneer Platform: It was Ethereum, the groundbreaking blockchain platform introduced by Vitalik Buterin, that played a pivotal role in the development of NFTs. Ethereum's smart contract functionality enabled the creation of NFTs, allowing digital assets to be tokenized, verified, and traded on the blockchain. This monumental shift paved the way for NFTs to move from concept to reality.

The First NFTs: The CryptoKitties phenomenon in 2017 marked the introduction of NFTs to a wider audience. These collectable digital cats took the world by storm, showcasing the potential of NFTs to represent unique, tradable assets in a virtual space. The success of CryptoKitties opened the floodgates for various industries to explore NFTs.

Art and NFTs: A Perfect Match: One of the earliest sectors to embrace NFTs was the art world. Artists saw an opportunity to digitize their creations, proving ownership and provenance through NFTs. The artist Beeple, for instance, made headlines in 2021 with his NFT artwork sale for a record-breaking $69 million at Christie's auction house. This spectacular event ushered NFTs into the mainstream and forever changed the way we perceive and trade art.

NFT Boom and Pop Culture: The NFT market boomed as the broader cultural zeitgeist latched onto the concept. Celebrities, musicians, and athletes joined the NFT craze, releasing exclusive digital content, music, and sports memorabilia as NFTs. This cultural shift signified the diversification of NFT use cases beyond art, demonstrating their capacity to redefine value across multiple sectors.

Digital Real Estate and NFTs: NFTs are not limited to the intangible world. The real estate industry saw the potential of NFTs to revolutionize property ownership. Real estate NFTs represent ownership of physical properties and open doors for fractional ownership and decentralized finance in the property market. This intersection of the physical and digital worlds was a significant milestone in the NFT journey.

CryptoPunks and the Age of Collectibles: In the ever-evolving world of NFTs, the concept of "collectables" gained prominence. CryptoPunks, a collection of 10,000 unique 24x24 pixel art characters, was one of the pioneering NFT collectables. The rarity of these characters, coupled with their unique attributes, led to a thriving secondary market where collectors could buy, sell, and trade their digital "punks."

NFTs in the Gaming Universe: NFTs found fertile ground in the gaming world, offering players a tangible digital asset that could be bought, sold, and traded. From virtual land parcels to in-game items, the gaming industry adopted NFTs as a way to enhance player experiences and potentially monetize in-game assets. NFTs made digital possessions more than just ephemeral virtual goods.

NFTs Beyond Borders: NFTs have transcended geographical boundaries, connecting creators and collectors from all corners of the globe. This borderless characteristic has encouraged collaboration, creativity, and new perspectives in the NFT ecosystem. Artists and creators are no longer restricted by geographical constraints, as their work can be shared and appreciated worldwide through NFTs.

Tokenization of Intellectual Property: NFTs expanded into the realm of intellectual property, enabling creators to assert their rights and receive royalties in an immutable and transparent manner. Authors, musicians, and filmmakers have begun to tokenize their work, ensuring that they continue to benefit from their creations in the digital age.

The Advent of NFT Marketplaces: NFT marketplaces, such as OpenSea, Rarible, and SuperRare, provide the infrastructure for creators and collectors to connect, trade, and build communities. These platforms offer user-friendly interfaces, making it accessible for individuals to buy and sell NFTs with ease. They have become hubs for exploring the vast NFT landscape.

Legal Framework and Challenges: As NFTs continue to grow, they have encountered a range of legal and ethical challenges, from copyright issues to environmental concerns related to energy-intensive blockchain networks. Addressing these challenges is essential for the sustainable development of NFTs and their coexistence with traditional legal systems.

The Evolution Continues: The journey of NFTs from their humble beginnings to their current state is nothing short of astonishing. It's a journey that transcends technology and finance, touching art, entertainment, gaming, and more. With NFTs constantly evolving, the future holds endless possibilities, and the magic of wealth creation through these digital tokens is just beginning.

As we navigate through the chapters of this book, we will delve deeper into the various facets of NFTs and how they have transformed the way we create, own, and exchange wealth in the digital era. So, fasten your seatbelts and get ready for an exciting voyage into the potent magic of wealth with NFTs, where the story is still being written.

Understanding NFTs

NFTs, or Non-Fungible Tokens, represent a significant leap in the world of digital assets. To truly comprehend their intricate workings, one must venture beyond the surface-level understanding and delve into their technical nuances. At first glance, the concept might seem perplexing, even daunting, with its labyrinth of technical jargon and blockchain complexities. However, once we peel back the layers and demystify the underlying mechanics, a world of limitless possibilities and wealth creation comes into focus.

NFTs, in their essence, are unique digital assets authenticated by blockchain technology, making them one-of-a-kind and irreplaceable. Unlike their fungible counterparts, such as cryptocurrencies, NFTs are indivisible and cannot be exchanged on a one-to-one basis. Each NFT carries a distinctive set of metadata that serves as its digital fingerprint, setting it apart from any other token in existence. This unique characteristic not only confers ownership but also confers a sense of exclusivity and scarcity, often driving their monetary value skyward.

The blockchain often likened to an immutable digital ledger, lies at the core of NFT functionality. Through the utilization of smart contracts, the blockchain enables the creation, verification, and secure transaction of NFTs without the need for intermediaries. These smart contracts operate as self-executing digital agreements, enforcing predefined rules and conditions, thereby ensuring transparency and trust between the parties involved. This decentralized nature of blockchain technology underpins the integrity and authenticity of NFT transactions, establishing a robust foundation for the burgeoning NFT ecosystem.

Immersing oneself in the world of NFTs requires a comprehensive understanding of the underlying technology that facilitates their existence. The process of minting NFTs involves the creation of a unique digital asset and its subsequent linkage to a specific blockchain network. This linkage, through the utilization of cryptographic hashing algorithms, imbues the NFT with its distinct identity and cryptographic integrity, safeguarding it from any potential tampering or fraudulent replication.

Key to the comprehension of NFTs is the notion of digital ownership and the transfer of this ownership across a decentralized network. The cryptographic keys associated with each NFT serve as the digital signatures of ownership, validating the authenticity of the asset and its rightful proprietor. Through these cryptographic keys, individuals can securely buy, sell, or trade NFTs on various online marketplaces, fostering a vibrant economy of digital collectables, artworks, and virtual assets.

One of the most intriguing aspects of NFTs lies in their programmability, allowing creators to embed specific functionalities and attributes within the token itself. These programmable features can range from royalty mechanisms that automatically distribute profits to the original creator with each subsequent sale, to access control mechanisms that regulate the usage rights of the NFT. This inherent versatility of NFTs offers an unprecedented level of customization and control, empowering creators and collectors alike to personalize their digital assets according to their unique preferences and requirements.

Furthermore, the interoperability of NFTs with different blockchain networks broadens their potential applications across diverse industries and use cases. This interoperability enables the seamless transfer of NFTs between various platforms, expanding their reach and accessibility to a wider audience. As a result, NFTs have found their way into domains such as art, music, gaming, virtual real estate, and even the metaverse, redefining the boundaries of digital ownership and creative expression.

However, with the proliferation of NFTs, concerns about environmental sustainability and energy consumption have garnered significant attention. The energy-intensive nature of certain blockchain networks, particularly those employing proof-of-work consensus mechanisms, has raised questions about the carbon footprint associated with NFT transactions. Efforts to address these environmental concerns have led to the exploration of alternative consensus mechanisms, such as proof-of-stake, which offer a more energy-efficient approach to validating blockchain transactions.

In the realm of NFTs, the concept of authenticity reigns supreme. The provenance of a digital asset, along with its immutable record of ownership, establishes a narrative of legitimacy and value. NFTs have the power to revolutionize the authentication process for digital artworks, collectables, and intellectual properties, providing a verifiable chain of custody that instils confidence and trust among potential buyers and collectors.

Moreover, the emerging trend of fractional ownership within the NFT space has unlocked new avenues for investment and wealth creation. Fractional ownership enables multiple investors to collectively own a share of an expensive NFT, thereby reducing the barrier to entry for high-value assets and allowing a broader demographic to participate in the NFT market. This democratization of ownership has the potential to democratize wealth generation, making lucrative investment opportunities more accessible and inclusive.

In conclusion, the realm of NFTs is a multifaceted landscape brimming with technical intricacies and transformative potential. By comprehending the fundamental mechanisms underpinning NFTs, one can harness their power to reshape traditional notions of ownership, creativity, and financial empowerment. NFTs represent not just a technological advancement but a paradigm shift in the way we perceive and interact with digital assets, offering a gateway to an era of unparalleled creativity and wealth generation.

NFTs in the Art World

The art world has long been a realm of innovation and transformation, where creativity knows no bounds. In recent years, the arrival of NFTs has brought about a revolution in the art market, forging an unbreakable bond between the traditional and the digital. This chapter is a journey into the mesmerizing marriage of art and blockchain, revealing the artists, collectors, and masterpieces that have rewritten the rules of the art world.

The Digital Renaissance

The art world is no stranger to change. It has seen the birth of new movements, the fall of old institutions, and the rise of unconventional artists who dared to redefine the boundaries of creativity. NFTs have ushered in a digital renaissance, providing artists with the tools to embrace a new era of artistic expression.

In the digital realm, artists can create, tokenize, and sell their work as NFTs, ensuring that they retain control over their creations, and often, a share of the future profits when their art is resold. This newfound autonomy is revolutionary, as it empowers artists to navigate the art world without the need for traditional gatekeepers.

Collecting in the Digital Age

Art collectors have also been drawn into the vortex of this digital transformation. The allure of owning a unique, provably scarce digital asset has captivated collectors worldwide. As a result, they have ventured into the NFT space, seeking both new forms of art and investment opportunities.

Famous collectors, including celebrities and entrepreneurs, have joined the NFT art movement, further validating the legitimacy and potential of NFTs in the art world. The likes of Beeple's "Everyday: The First 5000 Days" selling for millions have piqued the interest of traditional art collectors and investors.

The Art of Tokenization

The process of tokenization lies at the heart of NFTs in the art world. Artists take their creations and tokenize them as NFTs, effectively transforming their work into a unique, indivisible, and immutable digital asset on the blockchain. This enables artists to represent their art in a way that has never been possible before, allowing them to define its rarity, provenance, and ownership in an unforgeable manner.

For collectors, the ownership of an NFT represents not just a digital image but a certificate of authenticity, ownership, and a direct connection with the artist. It's a whole new way of collecting art, transcending the constraints of physicality.

Breaking Boundaries and Empowering Creators

NFTs have become a powerful tool for artists to explore previously uncharted territories, transcending geographical and cultural boundaries. Artists no longer need to rely on traditional art institutions or galleries to gain recognition. NFT platforms provide an open, global stage where artists can showcase their work to a vast and diverse audience.

This newfound accessibility has led to an unprecedented diversification in the art world. Emerging and underrepresented artists can now find their niche and gain a following, without facing the barriers imposed by the traditional art market.

Famous NFT Art Sales

NFTs have thrust both established and emerging artists into the spotlight. A notable example is Beeple, whose digital artwork "Everyday: The First 5000 Days" sold at a Christie's auction for an astounding $69 million, catapulting him to the pinnacle of art and NFT history.

Crypto-art pioneer CryptoPunks, an early NFT project, continues to capture attention and has seen individual punks sell for hundreds of thousands of dollars. These unique 24x24 pixel art characters have left an indelible mark on the NFT art landscape.

Similarly, the CryptoKitties craze brought blockchain-based digital collectables to the fore, allowing users to breed and trade virtual cats. The concept may sound whimsical, but it demonstrates the potential of NFTs to blend creativity and commerce.

Emerging Artists and the NFT Revolution

While established artists have certainly embraced NFTs, it is the emerging talents who have witnessed a meteoric rise through these digital tokens. Digital artists, in particular, have found a welcoming space in the NFT world. They have leveraged their digital skills to create art that resonates with a new generation of collectors.

NFTs have unlocked the path for unknown artists to gain recognition and financial success. It's no longer about who you know or where you are from; it's about the quality and uniqueness of your work.

Artistic Collaboration and Community

NFTs have also fostered an environment of collaboration and community among artists. Collaborative pieces, where multiple artists contribute to a single NFT project, have become a common and celebrated practice. This sense of unity and shared creativity has propelled NFT art into a realm of its own.

Furthermore, NFT art communities have flourished, with artists and collectors connecting on social media and dedicated NFT platforms. Artists can receive instant feedback from their audience and engage with their collectors in a way that transcends traditional gallery settings.

The Ethereal World of Virtual Galleries

Virtual galleries have sprung up in the digital landscape, providing an immersive experience for art lovers. These galleries offer a bridge between the physical and digital worlds, enabling users to explore NFT art in a three-dimensional setting.

Virtual reality (VR) technology has taken this concept even further, offering a fully immersive experience where users can stroll through digital art spaces and interact with the artworks themselves. The result is an enchanting, otherworldly experience that brings art to life.

NFT Art Beyond the Visual

While NFT art is often associated with visual pieces, it extends beyond the realm of traditional painting and illustration. Musicians and other audio artists have entered the scene, using NFTs to tokenize music and sound. Even literary works have found their place in the NFT world, providing a platform for authors to sell limited-edition digital copies of their books.

This expansion of the NFT art world showcases the versatility and adaptability of blockchain technology in serving creators of all kinds.

Challenges and Controversies

As with any transformative movement, the intersection of NFTs and art has not been without its challenges and controversies. Environmental concerns have been raised due to the energy-intensive nature of blockchain technology. Additionally, issues related to copyright and plagiarism in the NFT art world have sparked debates about authenticity and ownership.

The ethereal nature of digital art has also raised questions about its long-term value and preservation. How can art be preserved for generations when it exists solely in the digital realm?

The Path Forward

Despite these challenges, the NFT art movement continues to evolve, adapt, and inspire. It has opened doors for artists, collectors, and art enthusiasts, creating a dynamic space where innovation and creativity thrive.

In the next chapter, we will delve deeper into the impact of NFTs in the entertainment industry, exploring how musicians, filmmakers, and content creators are harnessing this transformative technology to shape the future of their respective industries. The NFT journey has only just begun, and its potential to transform wealth and creativity knows no bounds.

NFTs in the Entertainment Industry

The entertainment industry, with its vibrant tapestry of music, film, and creative art forms, has long been a bastion of innovation and imagination. With the advent of Non-Fungible Tokens (NFTs), this landscape is undergoing a digital renaissance that is transforming the way creators interact with their fans and how revenue streams are forged.

1. The Digital Evolution of Creativity

The entertainment industry's embrace of NFTs signifies a significant shift in the way artists and creators are approaching their craft. These digital tokens are like keys to a realm where the traditional boundaries of ownership, distribution, and engagement are being rewritten.

2. Musicians and NFTs: A Harmonious Revolution

Musicians have found a profound resonance with NFTs. For artists, these tokens open doors to new possibilities. They can release limited edition albums, unique tracks, or concert tickets as NFTs, thereby creating an intimate connection with their fans while establishing a sustainable source of revenue.

3. Film Industry and NFTs: Scripting New Opportunities

In the world of cinema, NFTs are no less transformative. Independent filmmakers, studios, and even actors are exploring the potential of tokenizing film rights, collectables, and exclusive premiere experiences. NFTs provide a novel way for film enthusiasts to own a piece of their favourite movies.

4. Content Creators and NFTs

Beyond traditional entertainment domains, content creators on platforms like YouTube, TikTok, and Instagram are also leveraging NFTs. By tokenizing their content, they offer fans exclusive access, special privileges, or even a share of the creator's future success. It's a collaborative venture between artists and their audiences, underpinned by trust and creativity.

5. The New Artistic Connection

The connection between artists and their audiences has always been a vital element of the entertainment industry. NFTs enhance this connection by offering fans the chance to own a piece of the artist's work, and in doing so, they become stakeholders in the creative process.

6. Rarity and Exclusivity

One of the key attractions of NFTs in the entertainment industry is the concept of rarity and exclusivity. Artists can release limited editions or unique collectables as NFTs, making them highly sought after by collectors and fans. This scarcity often drives up the value of these digital assets.

7. The Advent of Smart Contracts

Smart contracts underpin NFTs, automating royalty payments for artists. When a fan resells an NFT at a higher price, a portion of the proceeds can be automatically directed back to the creator, ensuring a consistent revenue stream over time.

8. Unlocking Monetization in Gaming

Gaming and entertainment are becoming increasingly intertwined, and NFTs are a bridge between these worlds. Gamers can trade in-game assets as NFTs, and game developers can offer limited-edition virtual items. This dynamic not only enhances the gaming experience but also opens up new avenues for wealth generation in the industry.

9. From Fan to Patron

NFTs redefine the role of fans as mere spectators. They can now become patrons and collectors, investing in their favourite artists or creators. This shift in dynamics fosters a deeper sense of loyalty and engagement.

10. Virtual Reality and NFTs

Virtual reality experiences are another frontier where NFTs are gaining traction. Creators can tokenize virtual real estate, items, and experiences within these immersive environments, thereby adding a layer of value and ownership to the digital realm.

11. The Art of Tokenization

The process of creating NFTs is often viewed as an art form in itself. Artists and creators meticulously craft their tokens, imbuing them with unique qualities that resonate with their audiences.

12. Legal and Copyright Implications

The intersection of NFTs and intellectual property rights is a subject of ongoing debate and legal scrutiny. As NFTs challenge the traditional notions of ownership, artists and creators need to navigate the legal complexities to protect their work and interests.

13. The Fan-Driven Marketplace

NFT marketplaces are vibrant hubs where fans, collectors, and creators converge. They form a close-knit community where the appreciation of art, music, and entertainment takes on new dimensions, transcending geographical boundaries.

14. Challenges and Opportunities

NFTs present both challenges and opportunities for the entertainment industry. The industry must grapple with questions of environmental sustainability and inclusion while also benefiting from the innovative revenue streams that NFTs offer.

15. A Collaborative Future

The journey of NFTs in the entertainment industry is a collaborative one. Creators, fans, and technologists are together exploring this uncharted territory, creating a new paradigm that promises to be richer, more interactive, and more rewarding for all involved.

In the world of entertainment, NFTs are the threads that weave together the fabric of the digital age. The embrace of these tokens is not just a trend; it's a profound transformation that is reshaping the way we consume, experience, and engage with music, film, art, and creativity itself. As the entertainment industry continues to adapt to this digital revolution, the power of NFTs to redefine relationships with fans and revenue streams is only beginning to unfold. The magic of wealth creation through NFTs is a captivating tale that is still being written, and it promises to be a masterpiece of our times.

NFTs in Gaming

The world of gaming has always been a realm of imagination and excitement, where players immerse themselves in virtual landscapes, battling foes and exploring fantastical realms. However, with the advent of Non-Fungible Tokens (NFTs), gaming has transcended its traditional boundaries, ushering in a new era of ownership and value within virtual ecosystems. Gaming enthusiasts now find themselves drawn into a dynamic universe where virtual assets hold tangible worth, and the possibilities seem boundless.

In this chapter, we plunge headfirst into the enthralling intersection of NFTs and the gaming industry. No longer confined to mere virtual experiences, gamers now possess the opportunity to truly own their in-game items, from legendary weapons to rare skins and coveted collectables. These digital assets, represented as NFTs on blockchain platforms, have unlocked a fresh dimension of value and ownership, revolutionizing the very essence of gaming as we know it.

NFTs in gaming have breathed life into the concept of digital ownership, allowing players to invest in unique, one-of-a-kind virtual items that hold intrinsic value within their respective game universes. By leveraging blockchain technology, these assets are securely recorded on decentralized ledgers, guaranteeing authenticity and provenance. This newfound sense of ownership empowers gamers, fostering a deeper connection to their virtual avatars and possessions, transcending the conventional boundaries between the real and the digital.

Moreover, the integration of NFTs in gaming has fueled the rise of decentralized gaming economies, where players can trade, buy, and sell their digital assets directly within the gaming ecosystem. This seamless integration not only fosters a vibrant marketplace within the game but also provides players with the opportunity to generate real wealth through the acquisition and exchange of valuable in-game items.

The concept of play-to-earn has become a pivotal component within the NFT gaming landscape. Players can now monetize their skills and achievements, earning tangible rewards for their in-game accomplishments. This innovative approach has redefined the traditional notion of gaming, transforming it into a viable source of income and financial empowerment for skilled and dedicated players.

Furthermore, NFTs have catalyzed the development of unique gaming experiences, offering players exclusive access to limited-edition content, special events, and personalized in-game experiences. These exclusive offerings not only enhance the overall gaming experience but also cultivate a sense of exclusivity and prestige, driving unparalleled engagement and loyalty within the gaming community.

The introduction of NFTs has also instigated a paradigm shift in the gaming industry, as game developers and publishers now prioritize the integration of NFTs within their gaming ecosystems. This strategic shift has not only bolstered the revenue streams of game developers but has also enabled them to foster a more symbiotic relationship with their player base, incentivizing active participation and engagement through the creation and acquisition of NFT-based assets.

Additionally, NFTs in gaming have initiated a collaborative culture within the gaming community, where players actively participate in the creation and curation of in-game content. This participatory approach fosters a sense of community and inclusivity, as players contribute to the development of the virtual world, co-creating an immersive gaming experience that reflects their collective vision and creativity.

The integration of NFTs has also paved the way for cross-platform interoperability, enabling players to utilize their virtual assets across multiple games and platforms seamlessly. This interconnected gaming ecosystem not only amplifies the utility and value of in-game assets but also promotes a sense of continuity and flexibility, allowing players to explore diverse virtual environments while retaining ownership of their prized NFT possessions.

Moreover, the rise of blockchain-based gaming has introduced a transparent and secure environment for players, eliminating the risks associated with fraudulent transactions and counterfeit in-game items. The immutable nature of blockchain technology ensures that each transaction and asset transfer is recorded and verified, mitigating the possibility of fraud and safeguarding the integrity of the gaming economy.

Furthermore, the integration of NFTs has facilitated the emergence of dynamic gaming communities, where players engage in collaborative gameplay experiences, virtual events, and communal challenges. This vibrant social landscape fosters camaraderie and camaraderie, as players band together to achieve common goals, unlock exclusive rewards, and shape the evolving narrative of their favourite virtual worlds.

In conclusion, the marriage of NFTs and the gaming industry has unleashed a wave of transformative possibilities, revolutionizing the way gamers interact with virtual assets and redefining the essence of digital ownership. As NFTs continue to weave their way into the fabric of gaming, they not only enhance the overall gaming experience but also empower players with newfound avenues for creativity, collaboration, and financial empowerment within the immersive realms of virtual gaming.

NFTs in Real Estate

The world of Non-Fungible Tokens (NFTs) isn't confined to the digital landscape alone; it's making its presence felt in the age-old realm of real estate, one of the most enduring forms of wealth. In this chapter, we will embark on a journey to explore how NFTs are orchestrating a digital transformation in the real estate market, offering a glimpse into the promising future of this traditional industry.

The Dawn of a New Era

The concept of owning a piece of property has always been synonymous with tangible, brick-and-mortar assets. However, the advent of NFTs has given rise to a paradigm shift, where ownership is not bound by physical presence but is symbolized through digital tokens. These tokens, representing real estate assets, have the potential to revolutionize the way we buy, sell, and invest in properties.

Tokenizing Real Estate Assets

The process begins with tokenization – converting a real estate asset into NFTs. This transformation divides ownership into smaller, more manageable units, making it accessible to a wider range of investors. A single property can be split into numerous tokens, allowing fractional ownership and democratising investment opportunities.

Accessibility and Liquidity

By breaking down ownership into smaller portions, NFTs make real estate investments more accessible. Individuals who may have been unable to invest in an entire property can now participate in the real estate market. Additionally, NFTs introduce a new level of liquidity to the real estate market, as tokens can be bought, sold, or traded with ease.

Global Reach

NFTs transcend geographical boundaries. They allow investors from around the world to engage in real estate investments without the need for extensive legal processes or physical presence. This global reach not only broadens the investor base but also brings a diverse range of perspectives and experiences to the real estate market.

Transparency and Security

The blockchain technology underlying NFTs ensures transparency and security in real estate transactions. Smart contracts, which execute automatically when predetermined conditions are met, eliminate intermediaries, reduce the risk of fraud, and simplify the buying and selling process. This newfound trust in the system is one of the cornerstones of the NFT revolution in real estate.

Unlocking Liquidity for Property Owners

Property owners also stand to benefit from NFTs. Those looking to unlock the value of their properties without selling them can do so by tokenizing and offering shares of their assets to a broader audience. This allows property owners to tap into liquidity without relinquishing complete control.

Diverse Investment Opportunities

NFTs in real estate open the door to diverse investment opportunities. You can invest in residential properties, commercial spaces, or even unique spaces like iconic landmarks. This diversification allows investors to curate their real estate portfolios according to their preferences and risk tolerance.

Enhanced Financing Options

NFTs provide a range of financing options for real estate development. Developers can raise capital by selling NFTs for projects under development, offering investors the chance to be a part of the journey from the ground up. This not only benefits developers but also encourages community involvement.

Unlocking Illiquid Assets

Illiquid assets, like high-value properties that are difficult to sell, can be tokenized and made accessible to a broader market. This unlocks the potential of otherwise stagnant assets, providing an innovative solution for property owners and investors.

Challenges and Regulations

Despite the tremendous potential, the integration of NFTs into real estate is not without its challenges. Regulatory frameworks, taxation, and the legal intricacies of real estate transactions need to evolve to accommodate this disruptive technology. Governments and authorities are navigating this new terrain, and it's an area to watch closely as the real estate-NFT landscape develops.

Navigating the NFT Real Estate Market

As with any investment, navigating the NFT real estate market requires a keen understanding of both NFT technology and the real estate industry. Due diligence, market research, and expert advice are essential to make informed investment decisions.

The Potential for Growth

NFTs have shown the potential to bring significant changes to the real estate market. The ability to democratize real estate investment, improve transparency, and create new financing options is attracting attention from investors and developers alike. While the market is still evolving, it is essential to stay informed about the latest developments and opportunities.

Real-World Examples

Several real estate projects have already embraced NFT technology. These pioneering initiatives are a testament to the transformative power of NFTs in the real estate market. Notable examples include the tokenization of landmark buildings, luxury homes, and even entire islands.

The Future of Real Estate with NFTs

The digital transformation of real estate through NFTs is still in its infancy, and the full extent of its impact is yet to be realized. As technology continues to advance and regulatory hurdles are overcome, we can anticipate a more vibrant, accessible, and secure real estate market powered by NFTs.

Conclusion

NFTs are not only revolutionizing the world of art, entertainment, and gaming, but they are also reshaping the traditional concept of real estate ownership. By making real estate more accessible, liquid, and secure, NFTs are democratizing wealth and changing the way we invest in property. While the industry is still in its early stages, the potential for NFTs to transform the real estate market is undeniable. As technology, regulations, and market adoption evolve, the future of real estate with NFTs holds great promise, offering new opportunities for investors and property owners alike.

Investment and Speculation

As we venture deeper into the world of NFTs, it becomes evident that they are not just a digital marvel but also a realm where the potential for wealth creation is vast. However, like any innovative domain, NFTs come with their own set of challenges and complexities. In this chapter, we will delve into the intriguing aspects of investment and speculation within the NFT landscape.

1. The Allure of NFT Investment

NFTs have captured the imaginations of many as a new avenue for investment. The allure lies in the ability to own unique digital assets that can be appreciated over time. Unlike traditional investments, NFTs offer a tangible connection to the digital world, which is becoming increasingly significant.

2. The Power of Digital Ownership

NFTs represent a paradigm shift in ownership. Owning an NFT isn't just about having access to a digital file; it's about owning a unique, verified token on the blockchain. This novel form of digital ownership has sparked the interest of collectors and investors alike.

3. Diversification with NFTs

Investors have recognized the value of diversifying their portfolios with NFTs. These digital assets provide a unique opportunity to spread risk across different classes of collectables, art, virtual real estate, and more, thereby enhancing the diversity of one's investment portfolio.

4. Speculation: The Double-Edged Sword

While investment in NFTs holds great promise, it is essential to acknowledge the speculative nature of this domain. Prices of NFTs can be highly volatile, and the market can experience sudden fluctuations. Speculation can be rewarding but also risky.

5. The Rollercoaster Ride

The world of NFT investment resembles a rollercoaster ride, with exhilarating highs and stomach-churning lows. Prices can skyrocket when a notable NFT is sold, and then plummet when the market cools down. It's crucial to be prepared for these price swings.

6. The Rarity Factor

One of the factors that make NFTs valuable is rarity. Scarce NFTs, such as those from renowned artists or limited-edition collectables, often fetch exorbitant prices in the market. Rarity has become synonymous with value in the NFT world.

7. Investment Strategies

As with any investment, having a well-thought-out strategy is paramount. NFT investors must consider factors such as their risk tolerance, investment horizon, and objectives. Developing a clear strategy can help mitigate the risks associated with speculation.

8. The Hype Cycle

NFT markets are susceptible to the hype cycle, where intense interest and investment drive prices to unprecedented levels, only to be followed by a sudden correction. Staying informed and understanding market trends is crucial to navigate these cycles successfully.

9. Due Diligence

In the NFT world, due diligence is a critical step. Conduct thorough research about the NFT, its creator, and its history before investing. Ensure that the NFT is legitimate and not a copy or forgery.

10. NFT Price Factors

Several factors can impact the price of an NFT, including the reputation of the creator, the uniqueness of the digital asset, the demand from collectors and investors, and the broader sentiment in the NFT market. It's vital to consider these elements when evaluating an NFT's investment potential.

11. Investment Timeframe

Different NFTs may have varying investment horizons. Some NFTs may offer quick returns, while others might be long-term investments. Deciding on your investment timeframe can help you tailor your approach to the NFT market.

12. Navigating Market Fluctuations

Being prepared for market fluctuations is crucial. Diversification, setting stop-loss orders, and not overextending yourself are essential strategies to protect your investments during turbulent times.

13. The Emotional Aspect

Investing in NFTs can evoke strong emotions. Prices can surge to astonishing heights, but they can also plummet. Emotional control is a valuable asset for NFT investors, allowing them to make rational decisions in a highly charged environment.

14. Seek Professional Advice

As the NFT market continues to evolve, seeking professional advice can be a wise move, especially for those new to the domain. Experts can provide insights, guide your investment decisions, and help you navigate the complexities of the NFT landscape.

15. The Future of NFT Investment

The NFT landscape is continually evolving, presenting new opportunities and challenges for investors and speculators. Keeping a keen eye on market developments and being adaptable to change will be key to staying ahead in the world of NFT investment.

In the exciting, yet volatile, world of NFTs, the line between investment and speculation blurs, making it a thrilling, yet unpredictable, domain. Success in NFT investment hinges on knowledge, diligence, and a willingness to adapt to the ever-changing market conditions. As we move forward, the landscape of NFTs is sure to offer a wealth of opportunities for those willing to explore the boundaries of digital ownership and value.

The Dark Side of NFTs

The meteoric rise of Non-Fungible Tokens (NFTs) has undoubtedly brought a wave of excitement and potential for wealth creation. However, like any innovation, the realm of NFTs is not without its shadows. As we delve into the ethical, environmental, and legal implications surrounding NFTs, it becomes evident that this digital phenomenon isn't entirely without its challenges. While NFTs open new avenues for creators and investors, their impact on the environment, issues of authenticity, and legal concerns raise questions that demand our attention and contemplation.

The Ethical Quandary Within the NFT space, ethical considerations have emerged, particularly surrounding the authenticity of digital artwork and the rights of creators. As NFTs enable the tokenization of digital art, concerns regarding plagiarism, copyright infringement, and ownership rights have come to the forefront. The lack of clear regulations and the ease of reproducing digital content have raised ethical questions about the protection of artists' intellectual property and the potential exploitation of their work in the digital landscape.

Environmental Concerns The environmental impact of NFTs has garnered significant attention, with critics raising alarms about the energy consumption associated with blockchain transactions. The process of minting, buying, and selling NFTs on certain platforms has been criticized for its significant carbon footprint, attributed to the energy-intensive proof-of-work consensus mechanism. As the NFT market expands, the need for sustainable practices and eco-friendly solutions becomes imperative to mitigate the environmental consequences of this digital revolution.

Legal Ambiguities The legal landscape surrounding NFTs is complex and multifaceted, presenting challenges related to intellectual property, taxation, and regulatory compliance. The absence of comprehensive legal frameworks tailored to NFTs has created uncertainties regarding the enforceability of contracts, the protection of digital assets, and the taxation of NFT transactions. Additionally, the international nature of the NFT market further complicates matters, necessitating global collaboration and cohesive regulatory standards to address the legal ambiguities within this burgeoning digital economy.

Transparency and Authenticity One of the fundamental issues facing the NFT ecosystem is the assurance of authenticity and provenance of digital assets. With the ease of creating and replicating digital content, ensuring the originality and uniqueness of NFTs becomes a crucial challenge. The lack of transparent verification processes has led to instances of fraudulent activity, undermining the trust and credibility of the entire NFT marketplace. Establishing robust verification protocols and blockchain-based authentication mechanisms is vital to foster transparency and build confidence among NFT creators, investors, and consumers.

Social Impact and Inclusivity While NFTs offer new avenues for wealth creation, there remains a concern about the accessibility and inclusivity of this digital economy. The barrier to entry, including the technical knowledge required to navigate blockchain technology and the initial investment needed to participate, may limit the opportunities available to a broader demographic. Fostering education, promoting inclusivity, and cultivating a supportive community within the NFT space is essential to ensuring that the benefits of this innovative technology are accessible to a diverse and global audience.

Market Volatility and Speculative Risks The volatile nature of the NFT market introduces speculative risks that may impact both creators and investors. Fluctuations in the value of digital assets, coupled with the unpredictability of market trends, can lead to financial instability and potential losses for those involved in NFT transactions. The absence of traditional valuation metrics and the influence of speculative trading practices underscore the need for informed decision-making and risk management strategies to navigate the ever-evolving NFT landscape.

Privacy and Data Security As NFT transactions involve the exchange of sensitive digital information, concerns regarding data security and privacy protection have become paramount. The risk of data breaches, identity theft, and unauthorized access to personal information poses a significant threat within the NFT ecosystem. Implementing robust data encryption protocols, fostering cybersecurity best practices, and adhering to stringent privacy regulations are critical to safeguarding the integrity and confidentiality of individuals' data within the digital marketplace.

Cultural and Societal Impact The proliferation of NFTs has sparked debates about their cultural and societal impact, particularly about the commodification of art and the transformation of cultural artefacts into tradable digital assets. The digitization of cultural heritage and its transformation into a speculative commodity raises concerns about the preservation of cultural identity and the commercialization of intangible heritage. Respecting cultural values, promoting responsible digital practices, and preserving the integrity of cultural artefacts are imperative to uphold the cultural and societal significance of NFTs.

Consumer Protection In the absence of comprehensive consumer protection measures, the vulnerability of buyers and sellers in the NFT marketplace is a pressing concern. Instances of fraudulent transactions, misrepresentation of digital assets, and disputes over ownership rights highlight the need for robust consumer protection policies tailored to the unique characteristics of NFT transactions. Implementing transparent transactional processes, fostering dispute-resolution mechanisms, and establishing consumer-centric guidelines is vital to safeguarding the interests of participants within the NFT ecosystem.

Regulatory Challenges Navigating the regulatory landscape surrounding NFTs presents a significant challenge, given the diverse and evolving nature of digital assets. The absence of standardized regulatory frameworks tailored to NFTs has created regulatory gaps and inconsistencies, leaving the market susceptible to potential risks and illicit activities. Collaborative efforts between industry stakeholders, regulatory authorities, and policymakers are essential to establishing comprehensive regulatory guidelines that promote market integrity, transparency, and investor protection within the NFT ecosystem.

Educational Initiatives Promoting educational initiatives and fostering digital literacy are essential components in addressing the challenges associated with NFTs. Enhancing public awareness of blockchain technology, NFT functionalities, and the associated risks and opportunities can empower individuals to make informed decisions within the digital marketplace. Investing in educational resources, workshops, and training programs geared towards NFT adoption and best practices can contribute to a more informed and responsible NFT community.

Community Governance Building a robust governance structure within the NFT community is crucial for fostering accountability, transparency, and trust among stakeholders. Establishing community-driven initiatives, governance protocols, and collaborative decision-making processes can facilitate open dialogue and collective problem-solving within the NFT ecosystem. Encouraging active participation, promoting ethical standards, and nurturing a culture of inclusivity and diversity is key to cultivating a resilient and sustainable NFT community.

Evolving Technological Solutions, the dynamic nature of blockchain technology necessitates continual innovation and technological advancements to address the challenges facing the NFT ecosystem. Implementing scalable solutions, enhancing blockchain infrastructure, and integrating sustainable practices can pave the way for a more efficient, secure, and eco-friendly NFT marketplace. Embracing technological evolution, fostering research and development, and promoting interdisciplinary collaboration are essential to shaping the future of NFTs in a way that is sustainable and responsible.

Collective Responsibility Addressing the dark side of NFTs requires a collective commitment from all stakeholders, including creators, investors, regulators, and technological innovators. Fostering a culture of responsibility, accountability, and ethical conduct within the NFT community is paramount to mitigating the challenges and risks associated with this emerging digital landscape. Embracing a collective sense of responsibility and upholding ethical standards can nurture a resilient and sustainable NFT ecosystem that fosters innovation, inclusivity, and positive social impact.

In navigating the complexities of the dark side of NFTs, it is imperative to approach these challenges with a holistic perspective that encompasses ethical, environmental, legal, and social considerations. By fostering a culture of transparency, responsibility, and innovation, we can cultivate an NFT ecosystem that not only unlocks the potential of digital wealth creation but also upholds the values of integrity, sustainability, and inclusivity. As we confront these challenges, we must embrace the opportunity to shape the future of NFTs in a manner that aligns with our collective vision for a more equitable, transparent, and sustainable digital economy.

NFT Communities

In the digital realm of Non-Fungible Tokens (NFTs), where innovation and creativity thrive, communities play an indispensable role. They are the lifeblood of this dynamic ecosystem, weaving together a diverse tapestry of individuals, artists, collectors, and enthusiasts. In this chapter, we embark on an exploration of the various NFT communities that have emerged, delving into their unique characteristics, shared passions, and the invaluable contributions they make to the collective growth of the NFT space.

1. The NFT Universe Unveiled

In the vast expanse of the NFT universe, communities are the constellations that guide enthusiasts to their niches and like-minded peers. These communities form around shared interests, be it digital art, virtual real estate, gaming, or even more niche passions like blockchain-inspired memes. They provide a sense of belonging and facilitate collaboration in this ever-evolving digital landscape.

2. Creators and Collectors Converge

One of the remarkable aspects of NFT communities is the convergence of creators and collectors. These spaces provide a platform for artists to connect directly with their audience, forging relationships that transcend geographical boundaries. Artists can gain valuable feedback, while collectors can access exclusive pieces and even participate in the creation process through collaborations.

3. Artistic Alchemy

NFT communities are often a hub for artists looking to explore the alchemical fusion of traditional and digital art. This is where the magic of NFTs truly shines, enabling artists to tokenize their creations, retain ownership, and receive royalties on secondary sales. As artists explore this new medium, these communities offer not only appreciation but also crucial support and mentorship.

4. Diverse Digital Realms

NFT communities span a spectrum of creative endeavours, including digital art, music, virtual real estate, and even virtual fashion. Each community brings a unique flavour, drawing in enthusiasts who share a passion for a specific aspect of NFTs. These diverse digital realms create an environment where every individual can find their niche.

5. The Power of Discord and Forums

While digital spaces for NFT communities can be found across various platforms, Discord and dedicated forums have become the epicentres of engagement. Here, enthusiasts come together to discuss trends, discover new artists, and partake in exclusive events and auctions. These spaces are akin to bustling town squares where ideas and creations are exchanged.

6. The Mentorship Network

NFT communities often act as mentorship networks. Newcomers can find guidance and advice from seasoned collectors and artists, helping them navigate the complexities of the NFT world. This mentorship fosters a sense of trust, making the journey into NFTs less daunting for those just starting.

7. Notable NFT Community Projects

Within the NFT community landscape, several notable projects stand out. The Bored Ape Yacht Club, Pudgy Penguins, and the Art Blocks Curators are just a few examples of communities that have garnered significant attention. These projects offer membership benefits, exclusivity, and a sense of belonging, making them highly sought after.

8. The Role of Curators

In some NFT communities, curators take on a pivotal role. These individuals are responsible for selecting and showcasing the best works within a given category, ensuring quality and uniqueness. This process aids collectors in making informed choices and drives the market forward.

9. The Social Fabric of NFTs

Communities are not just about transactions but also about forming meaningful connections. Many creators host social events, virtual galleries, and even real-world meetups, reinforcing the social fabric of NFTs. These gatherings foster friendships and collaborations that extend beyond the digital world.

10. The Impact of Tokenized Governance

Some NFT communities have embraced tokenized governance structures, enabling members to have a say in the direction and decisions of the community. Token holders can propose changes, vote on decisions, and actively shape the future of the community.

11. Philanthropy and Social Impact

NFT communities are not solely driven by financial gain; they also recognize the power of social impact. Many communities engage in philanthropic activities, such as donating to charitable causes or supporting artists in need. This altruistic dimension adds depth and purpose to the NFT movement.

12. Staying Informed and Updated

The NFT landscape is ever-evolving, with new projects, artists, and trends emerging regularly. NFT communities play a crucial role in keeping enthusiasts informed and updated. Members often share insights, market analysis, and news, helping everyone stay on top of the latest developments.

13. Cultivating Future Generations

NFT communities are not just about the present but also about the future. They actively encourage and mentor emerging artists, collectors, and enthusiasts. This ensures the sustainability of the NFT ecosystem, passing on knowledge and passion to the next generation.

14. NFTs as Cultural Catalysts

NFT communities are catalysts for cultural movements. They transcend geographical and cultural boundaries, fostering a global sense of unity and creativity. NFTs have the potential to redefine what art and creativity mean in the digital age, and communities are at the forefront of this transformation.

15. The Never-Ending Journey

In this ever-evolving NFT landscape, communities are not static entities. They grow, adapt, and evolve in tandem with the NFT space itself. As NFTs continue to redefine the financial and creative landscapes, these communities are the companions on an exciting, never-ending journey, where innovation and human connection intertwine to unlock the potent magic of wealth with NFTs.

NFT communities are more than just groups of like-minded individuals; they are the beating heart of this digital renaissance, uniting people from all walks of life under the shared banner of creativity, innovation, and a belief in the transformative power of NFTs. Whether you are an artist, collector, investor, or simply an enthusiast, these communities provide a space for you to explore, create, connect, and, most importantly, thrive in this vibrant and ever-evolving world of NFTs.

Creating and Selling NFTs

In this digital era, the art of creating and selling NFTs has emerged as a transformative force, democratizing the world of art, and even intangible assets. Whether you're a budding artist, an entrepreneur, or someone with a unique idea to bring to the NFT marketplace, this chapter will be your guiding light. Here, we will delve deep into the realm of creating and selling NFTs, sharing valuable insights, tips, tricks, and best practices that will empower you to unlock the immense potential of this remarkable technology.

1. The Genesis of NFT Creation

To begin your journey into the world of NFTs, it's crucial to comprehend the genesis of NFT creation. NFTs are based on blockchain technology, which provides a secure and transparent way to tokenize your digital assets. You can create NFTs from digital art, music, videos, virtual real estate, or virtually anything digital.

2. Choosing the Right Blockchain

When venturing into NFT creation, choosing the right blockchain is of utmost importance. Ethereum is the most popular choice, but others like Binance Smart Chain, Flow, and Tezos have also gained prominence. Consider factors like gas fees, transaction speed, and community support when making your selection.

3. Wallets and Cryptocurrency

To create and sell NFTs, you'll need a cryptocurrency wallet. Ensure it supports the blockchain you've chosen. You'll also need cryptocurrency to cover transaction fees. Familiarize yourself with how to fund and manage your wallet securely.

4. Minting Your NFTs

The process of minting NFTs involves transforming your digital asset into a unique token. Minting platforms like OpenSea, Rarible, and Mintable offer user-friendly interfaces to help you create NFTs. You'll upload your digital file, add relevant metadata, and set parameters like royalties.

5. Metadata Matters

Your NFT's metadata is its digital identity. It includes information like the title, description, attributes, and tags. Crafting compelling metadata can significantly impact the attractiveness of your NFT to potential buyers.

6. The Rarity Factor

One of the keys to success in the NFT marketplace is creating NFTs with rarity. Rarity can be achieved by limiting the number of editions, incorporating unique features, or collaborating with other artists or creators. The rarer the NFT, the more appealing it becomes to collectors.

7. Legal and Copyright Considerations

Before you mint an NFT, it's essential to understand the legal and copyright implications. Ensure you have the right to sell the digital asset, or you risk legal troubles. Registering your work with a copyright office can add an extra layer of protection.

8. Navigating the Minting Fees

Minting NFTs often comes with fees, and these can vary based on the blockchain and platform you use. It's crucial to understand these fees and factor them into your pricing strategy. Balancing affordability for buyers while covering your costs is an art in itself.

9. Smart Contracts and Royalties

When minting an NFT, you have the opportunity to set royalties. This means you'll earn a percentage of the resale value every time your NFT changes hands. Smart contracts on the blockchain facilitate this, ensuring you receive your share automatically.

10. Marketing and Promotion

Once your NFT is minted and listed, don't expect it to sell like hotcakes on its own. Effective marketing and promotion are essential. Use social media, NFT forums, and partnerships to get the word out about your NFTs. Building a community around your work can make a significant difference.

11. NFT Auctions and Drops

NFTs can be sold through auctions or drops. Auctions allow collectors to bid on your NFT, potentially driving up the price. Drops involve selling a set number of NFTs at a specific time, often generating hype and demand.

12. Collaborations and Partnerships

Collaborating with other artists, influencers, or brands can boost your NFT sales. It can expand your reach and introduce your work to new audiences. Cross-promotion is a win-win strategy in the NFT world.

13. Engaging with the NFT Community

Active participation in the NFT community can provide you with valuable insights and connections. Joining NFT Discord channels, attending virtual events, and engaging with fellow creators can help you stay updated and navigate this ever-evolving landscape.

14. The Art of Pricing

Pricing your NFTs is both an art and a science. Consider the rarity, demand, and current market trends. Be open to adjusting your prices as you gain more experience and insight into the market.

15. Staying Informed

The NFT landscape is dynamic, with trends, platforms, and technologies evolving rapidly. Staying informed is crucial to making informed decisions. Follow NFT news, read whitepapers, and engage in continuous learning to thrive in this exciting realm.

As you embark on your NFT creation and selling journey, remember that success may not come overnight. Patience, adaptability, and a genuine passion for your craft are your allies. The NFT marketplace is a world of limitless potential, where creativity, innovation, and wealth creation intertwine in a mesmerizing dance. May your creations captivate the digital world and open the doors to the potent magic of wealth with NFTs.

The NFT Marketplace

In the thrilling world of NFTs, one of the most vital hubs is the NFT marketplace. These digital platforms serve as bustling marketplaces where artists, creators, collectors, and investors converge to exchange their prized non-fungible tokens. They are the lifeblood of the NFT ecosystem, offering a rich tapestry of opportunities for those looking to dive into this dynamic universe.

1. The Marketplace Unveiled: NFT marketplaces are digital platforms where NFTs are bought, sold, and traded. They bring together creators and collectors, acting as intermediaries facilitating transactions within the blockchain. It's like an enchanting bazaar where digital treasures await discovery.

2. Leading Players: Several NFT marketplaces have risen to prominence, with each offering its unique set of features and specialities. Market leaders like OpenSea, Rarible, and SuperRare have attracted substantial attention, boasting extensive collections and thriving communities.

3. Exploring OpenSea: OpenSea, often referred to as the "eBay of NFTs," is one of the largest and most established NFT marketplaces. It is renowned for its vast selection of digital assets, ranging from art and collectables to virtual real estate. Its user-friendly interface and robust search functionalities make it a preferred choice for many.

4. Rarible - The Home of Digital Creators: Rarible is a platform with a strong emphasis on creativity. It offers a unique twist by allowing users to create their NFTs and engage in governance through RARI tokens. This marketplace is perfect for artists and creators looking to carve their niche in the NFT space.

5. SuperRare: SuperRare caters to the world of digital art with a focus on limited-edition digital assets. Collectors can acquire unique pieces of digital art, each individually authenticated on the blockchain. It's a place where the value of art meets the innovation of blockchain.

6. Finding Your Niche: When navigating NFT marketplaces, it's important to find your niche. Whether you're an art connoisseur, a collector of virtual real estate, or a gaming enthusiast, there's a marketplace tailored to your interests. Explore different platforms to discover the one that aligns with your passion.

7. User Experience: The user experience within these marketplaces is continually evolving, with platforms striving to improve their interface and features. You'll find easy-to-use filters, sorting options, and categories that help streamline your search for the perfect NFT.

8. Community and Engagement: Apart from buying and selling, NFT marketplaces host vibrant communities. These communities offer an invaluable opportunity to network, collaborate, and share insights with like-minded individuals who share your enthusiasm for NFTs.

9. Ethereum Dominance: The majority of NFT marketplaces operate on the Ethereum blockchain, as Ethereum was the pioneer in the NFT space. However, other blockchains like Binance Smart Chain and Flow are also making headway in the NFT marketplace domain.

10. Rarity and Scarcity: One of the intriguing aspects of NFTs is the notion of rarity and scarcity. These attributes can greatly influence the value of an NFT. When exploring marketplaces, keep an eye out for limited edition or one-of-a-kind items that may appreciate over time.

11. Wallet Integration: To participate in NFT marketplaces, you'll need a cryptocurrency wallet compatible with the platform. These wallets allow you to securely store your NFTs and facilitate transactions. Ensure you're using a reliable and secure wallet to safeguard your digital assets.

12. Bidding and Auctions: Many NFT marketplaces employ bidding and auction mechanisms, allowing participants to compete for coveted NFTs. This can add an element of excitement and intrigue to the purchasing process.

13. Secondary Sales: In addition to primary sales, NFT marketplaces also support secondary sales. This means that once you own an NFT, you can sell it again on the same platform or other compatible marketplaces, potentially profiting from the appreciation in value.

14. Education and Due Diligence: As with any financial endeavour, it's crucial to educate yourself and exercise due diligence when exploring NFT marketplaces. Research the platforms, understand their fee structures, and be aware of potential scams or fraud within the NFT space.

15. The Future of NFT Marketplaces: The landscape of NFT marketplaces is constantly evolving. New platforms are emerging, each with innovative features and specializations. The future promises further growth and diversification, making the NFT marketplace scene an exciting one to watch.

Navigating NFT marketplaces can be a thrilling adventure, offering a myriad of opportunities for both collectors and creators. With the right knowledge, a discerning eye, and a touch of creativity, you can find your place in this vibrant and transformative digital realm, where the magic of wealth creation through NFTs knows no bounds.

Case Studies

In this pivotal chapter, we embark on a journey through the real-world success stories of individuals and organizations who have masterfully harnessed the potential of Non-Fungible Tokens (NFTs) to accumulate remarkable wealth. These compelling case studies are more than just financial victories; they are inspirational narratives that vividly showcase the astounding capabilities of NFTs in creating tangible value and securing a prosperous future.

The Digital Art Maverick: Meet Sarah Hensley, a visionary digital artist whose story encapsulates the transformative power of NFTs in the art world. From the confines of her modest studio, Sarah dared to dream beyond the conventional art scene, seeking a way to unleash her creativity while maintaining autonomy over her work. With the advent of NFTs, Sarah found her digital haven, a realm where her art could transcend geographical boundaries and connect with a global audience hungry for innovation.

Through the process of tokenizing her stunning artworks as NFTs, Sarah discovered a newfound sense of liberation. No longer confined to the whims of traditional galleries and art critics, she seized control of her artistic destiny. Her decision to embrace NFTs not only enabled her to directly engage with her patrons but also provided her with a platform to showcase her work on her terms.

As she immersed herself in the world of blockchain technology, Sarah witnessed her creations take on a life of their own, acquiring value that transcended the conventional confines of the art market. The very act of minting her art as NFTs imbued her pieces with a sense of exclusivity, scarcity, and authenticity, elements that resonated deeply with her growing global audience.

In the NFT marketplace, Sarah found a community of like-minded individuals who appreciated the digital medium's potential to redefine art and its worth. With each successful NFT auction, her confidence soared, and her works fetched prices that surpassed her wildest expectations, solidifying her status as a trailblazing digital artist.

Sarah's journey serves as a beacon of hope for artists navigating the complexities of the modern art world. Her story highlights how NFTs can catalyze creative emancipation, propelling artists towards newfound recognition and financial empowerment. As her art continues to captivate the digital sphere, Sarah remains a testament to the boundless opportunities that await those willing to embrace the transformative magic of NFTs.

CryptoPioneers: In the enchanting narrative of the Smith family, the once unassuming adopters of blockchain technology, a remarkable journey unfolds. Their early foray into the world of Non-Fungible Tokens (NFTs) began with a cautious exploration, fueled by a blend of curiosity and a burgeoning belief in the transformative power of digital assets. What started as an experimental venture soon metamorphosed into an inspiring tale of financial triumph.

As the family delved deeper into the intricacies of NFTs, they recognized the potential of these unique digital assets to transcend the traditional boundaries of wealth creation. With meticulous research and an intuitive understanding of market trends, they strategically allocated their modest crypto holdings into carefully selected NFTs, harnessing the decentralized nature of blockchain technology to their advantage.

Their journey, though not without its challenges, was marked by moments of awe-inspiring growth and steadfast determination. Through calculated risks and shrewd investments in emerging digital art, collectables, and virtual real estate, the Smiths witnessed their portfolio blossom into a substantial testament to the transformative potential of NFTs.

Their story serves as a beacon of hope and inspiration, illustrating how ordinary individuals, armed with knowledge, foresight, and a sprinkle of audacity, can navigate the dynamic landscape of NFTs to secure long-term financial stability. It is a testament to the democratizing force of technology, enabling even those without substantial financial prowess to participate in the exciting realm of digital wealth generation.

In a world where the potential of NFTs is often obscured by jargon and speculation, the Smiths' journey serves as a reassuring reminder that with dedication, research, and a willingness to embrace the possibilities of the digital frontier, anyone can unlock the potent magic of wealth with NFTs. Their story stands as a testament to the extraordinary opportunities that await those willing to embark on this exhilarating journey into the world of decentralized, digital prosperity.

NFTs and Philanthropy: Renowned philanthropist David Carter, recognized globally for his unwavering commitment to humanitarian causes, made headlines when he embraced the transformative potential of Non-Fungible Tokens (NFTs) to drive meaningful change. With an astute understanding of the burgeoning NFT market, Carter masterfully harnessed the power of digital art and collectables to bolster his philanthropic efforts.

Carter's foray into the world of NFTs was not merely a quest for financial gain; rather, it was a strategic endeavour to leverage the burgeoning interest in digital assets for the greater good. Through meticulously curated and exclusive NFT collections, including digital artworks, limited edition virtual memorabilia, and one-of-a-kind multimedia experiences, Carter orchestrated a series of groundbreaking auctions that captivated both the art and blockchain communities.

The success of Carter's NFT auctions transcended conventional fundraising methods, providing a refreshing and innovative approach to mobilizing resources for various humanitarian initiatives. By tapping into the enthusiasm of NFT collectors and enthusiasts worldwide, Carter facilitated an unprecedented surge of financial support for diverse causes, ranging from global health initiatives and environmental conservation to education and social empowerment programs.

Beyond the monetary impact, Carter's NFT-driven philanthropy sparked a renewed sense of community engagement and social responsibility within the digital realm. His vision of using NFTs as a force for good resonated deeply with a generation seeking purpose-driven investment opportunities and ways to contribute positively to society.

Through his pioneering efforts, Carter exemplified how NFTs could transcend their commercial value and serve as instruments of positive change. His story stands as a testament to the transformative potential of NFTs, inspiring a new wave of socially conscious creators, collectors, and investors to channel their passion for digital assets towards impactful philanthropy. As NFTs continue to redefine the landscape of wealth creation, Carter's legacy remains a beacon of hope, illustrating that financial success and social impact can go hand in hand in the digital era.

The Gaming Visionary: In the bustling realm of virtual gaming, Lucas Rodriguez stands out as a trailblazing visionary. As the mastermind behind an innovative concept that intertwines Non-Fungible Tokens (NFTs) with the gaming universe, he has redefined the rules of engagement, propelling gamers into a world where virtual assets hold tangible value. With a passion for both gaming and blockchain technology, Rodriguez embarked on a mission to revolutionize the gaming landscape by infusing it with the groundbreaking potential of NFTs.

His brainchild was a virtual ecosystem that grants players true ownership of in-game assets, a concept previously unimaginable in the gaming world. By leveraging the unique features of NFTs, he enabled players to buy, sell, and trade exclusive in-game items, characters, and land, fostering a vibrant economy within the virtual universe. This transformation not only elevated the gaming experience to unprecedented heights but also opened up new avenues for wealth generation.

Through Rodriguez's visionary approach, players found themselves immersed in an environment where their digital conquests translated into real-world wealth accumulation. The acquisition of rare and coveted virtual possessions now held substantial financial value, allowing gamers to capitalize on their gaming prowess. Additionally, the introduction of a decentralized marketplace empowered developers to directly monetize their creations, fostering a dynamic ecosystem where creativity and entrepreneurship thrived.

Under Rodriguez's leadership, the virtual landscape evolved into a bustling marketplace where players and developers alike reaped the rewards of their digital endeavours. The integration of NFTs into the gaming experience not only amplified the excitement of virtual exploration but also transformed it into a viable avenue for wealth creation. His groundbreaking concept serves as a testament to the transformative power of NFTs, showcasing their potential to transcend boundaries and redefine the very fabric of digital entertainment and wealth accumulation. As Lucas Rodriguez continues to pioneer the convergence of gaming and NFTs, his legacy remains etched in the annals of virtual innovation, inspiring a new generation of gamers and developers to unlock the potent magic of wealth within the digital realm.

Real Estate Reinvented: Marianne Thornton, a visionary real estate agent with an unyielding passion for innovation, found herself at the crossroads of tradition and modernity in the ever-evolving world of property transactions. Faced with the challenges of a stagnant market and the growing demand for digitization, she set out on a quest to revolutionize the industry through the integration of Non-Fungible Tokens (NFTs).

Recognizing the transformative potential of NFTs, Marianne embarked on a journey that would redefine the way properties were bought and sold. By tokenizing real properties as NFTs, she effectively fractionalized ownership, enabling individuals to invest in fractions of high-value properties with ease. This pioneering move not only democratized access to real estate investments but also fostered a new era of financial inclusivity.

Through her innovative approach, Marianne introduced a seamless and transparent process that eliminated the intermediaries and paperwork traditionally associated with property transactions. Leveraging blockchain technology, she ensured the immutability and security of property records, instilling confidence and trust within her growing clientele.

As word of her groundbreaking methods spread, Marianne became a beacon of inspiration for aspiring real estate entrepreneurs seeking to navigate the intricate landscape of NFTs. Her success not only sparked a surge of interest in the integration of NFTs within the real estate market but also propelled a wave of technological adoption within the industry.

Today, Marianne Thornton stands as a testament to the boundless possibilities that emerge when traditional industries embrace digital innovation. Her unwavering determination and forward-thinking approach not only transformed the way real estate transactions were conducted but also paved the way for a future where the power of NFTs continues to unlock new realms of wealth creation within the real estate market.

These case studies vividly illustrate the diverse and potent applications of NFTs in different sectors, emphasizing that NFTs are not limited to any single domain but rather represent a transformative force with the potential to reshape multiple aspects of our lives. These real-life success stories serve as an invaluable source of inspiration and motivation for readers, offering insights and ideas for their own NFT journeys.

By studying the accomplishments of these pioneers, you will gain a deeper appreciation of the vast wealth-creating possibilities that NFTs offer. The lessons drawn from these tales of success will undoubtedly empower you to embark on your own NFT adventure with confidence and purpose, enabling you to unlock the magical potential of wealth with NFTs in your unique way.

NFTs and the Future of Wealth

As we gaze into the horizon of the digital era, it becomes increasingly clear that NFTs are poised to play an even more significant role in shaping the future of wealth creation. The potential impact of these unique digital assets is nothing short of revolutionary, and it holds the promise of both incredible opportunities and pressing challenges.

Opportunities Abound

1. **Tokenized Assets:** The concept of tokenization extends far beyond art and collectables. We can envision a future where real estate, stocks, and various assets become tokenized, democratizing access to investments for people worldwide. NFTs could enable fractional ownership, making it easier for individuals to diversify their portfolios.

2. **Inclusive Finance:** NFTs have the potential to bridge financial gaps, providing access to the unbanked and underbanked populations. With a smartphone and an internet connection, individuals from all corners of the world can participate in the global economy, thereby reducing financial inequality.

3. **Digital Economies:** As virtual worlds and digital communities expand, NFTs are becoming the currency of choice within these ecosystems. Entrepreneurs are already building virtual businesses, and users are earning NFTs by participating in these platforms. The lines between the digital and physical worlds will continue to blur, ushering in new opportunities for wealth creation.

4. **NFT Royalties:** The concept of royalties tied to NFTs ensures creators a share of the revenue each time their work changes hands. This could revolutionize the way artists, musicians, writers, and creators are compensated, fostering an environment that rewards original content.

Challenges to Address

1. **Environmental Concerns:** NFTs have faced scrutiny due to their environmental impact, particularly in terms of energy consumption. As we move forward, addressing these concerns and finding sustainable solutions will be crucial to maintaining the long-term viability of NFTs.

2. **Regulation:** Governments and regulatory bodies are starting to take an interest in the NFT space, and this could lead to increased oversight and taxation. Striking a balance between innovation and compliance will be a challenge that the NFT community must navigate.

3. **Scams and Frauds:** With the rapid growth of NFTs, bad actors are attracted to the space. Protecting users from scams and fraudulent activities will be an ongoing challenge, requiring vigilant efforts from both platforms and users.

4. **Market Volatility:** The NFT market has shown signs of extreme volatility, with prices of digital assets skyrocketing and plummeting within a short span. Investors need to exercise caution and conduct thorough due diligence to minimize risk.

The future of wealth creation with NFTs is an unfolding narrative, filled with promise and potential, but also marked by challenges that must be met with innovative solutions. As this remarkable journey continues, it is imperative to embrace the opportunities and address the challenges to ensure that NFTs become a powerful force for positive change in the financial landscape. The NFT ecosystem will evolve, adapt, and mature, ultimately shaping a new era of wealth creation that transcends the boundaries of the physical world.

NFTs in Your Life

The NFT revolution is not confined to the realms of art, entertainment, or the elite. NFTs are accessible to everyone, and they have the potential to play a significant role in your financial strategy, regardless of your background or interests. In this chapter, we will explore how NFTs can be seamlessly integrated into your life, providing opportunities for wealth creation and financial empowerment.

1. The Democratization of Wealth with NFTs

NFTs are the epitome of the democratization of wealth. They provide an opportunity for individuals from diverse backgrounds to participate in the digital economy. Unlike traditional investments, NFTs do not require substantial upfront capital, making them more inclusive and accessible to the masses.

2. Diversifying Your Portfolio with NFTs

Diversification is a fundamental principle of sound financial management. By adding NFTs to your investment portfolio, you can spread risk and tap into the potential for significant returns. Just as you might invest in stocks, bonds, or real estate, NFTs offer a unique asset class that can contribute to your financial stability and growth.

3. NFTs as a Store of Value

Many people consider NFTs as a store of value, akin to holding physical assets like gold. This is because NFTs can appreciate over time, offering a hedge against inflation and economic uncertainty. By strategically acquiring NFTs with strong fundamentals, you can preserve your wealth and potentially see it grow.

4. NFTs as Collectibles and Memorabilia

For those who are passionate about collecting, NFTs offer a digital version of the cherished hobby. Digital collectables, such as trading cards, virtual pets, and rare in-game items, can become valuable assets in your collection. These NFTs not only bring joy but also the potential for financial gain.

5. NFTs in Gaming and Virtual Worlds

If you're an avid gamer, you can explore the integration of NFTs within your favourite virtual worlds. Games like Axie Infinity and Decentraland allow you to earn NFT assets that you can trade, sell, or use within the game ecosystem. Your in-game achievements can translate into tangible digital assets.

6. NFTs as a Source of Passive Income

NFTs can be a source of passive income. Some NFTs, like virtual real estate parcels in virtual worlds, can generate rent or lease income. This income can contribute to your financial stability and offer an additional revenue stream, all facilitated by the blockchain.

7. NFTs for Artists and Creators

If you're an artist, musician, writer, or any type of content creator, NFTs offer an exciting avenue to monetize your work directly. By tokenizing your creations as NFTs, you can reach a global audience and receive royalties each time your NFT is resold. This empowers artists to have more control over their work and financial destiny.

8. NFTs in Education and Certification

NFTs can also play a role in education and certification. Universities and institutions are exploring the use of NFTs to issue digital diplomas and certificates, ensuring the authenticity and immutability of academic achievements. This innovation can streamline the verification process and bolster your credentials.

9. NFTs for Charitable Causes

Engaging in philanthropy is a noble endeavour, and NFTs can be used to support charitable causes. Some NFT projects donate a portion of their proceeds to charitable organizations, allowing you to contribute to important causes while also potentially benefiting financially.

10. NFTs for Entrepreneurship

Entrepreneurs can leverage NFTs to fund their startups or innovative projects. By creating NFTs that represent shares in a venture or project, you can raise capital from a global pool of investors. This decentralizes the fundraising process and fosters innovation.

11. NFTs for Digital Identity and Authentication

NFTs can be used for digital identity and authentication. They can serve as digital passports, ensuring the authenticity of online profiles and accounts. This enhances online security and helps protect your digital presence.

12. NFTs for Intellectual Property Rights

If you're an inventor, author, or content creator, NFTs can play a pivotal role in protecting your intellectual property rights. By tokenizing your creations as NFTs, you can establish clear ownership and trace the usage of your work, potentially leading to licensing and royalty opportunities.

13. NFTs for Personal Branding

Building a personal brand is essential in today's digital age. NFTs can be used to create unique digital assets representing your brand. These assets can be traded, showcased, or even used as promotional tools, amplifying your online presence.

14. NFTs as a Learning Opportunity

Embracing NFTs in your life can also be a valuable learning opportunity. Understanding blockchain technology, smart contracts, and the dynamics of NFT markets can expand your knowledge in the rapidly evolving digital landscape.

15. Joining NFT Communities

NFT communities are welcoming and supportive of newcomers. Joining NFT-related forums, social media groups, and events can connect you with like-minded individuals and provide valuable insights and resources for your NFT journey.

In conclusion, NFTs offer a plethora of opportunities to integrate digital wealth into your life. Whether you're an artist, a gamer, an investor, an entrepreneur, or simply curious about the NFT space, there's a place for you in this exciting revolution. As NFTs continue to evolve and shape the future of finance, embracing them as a part of your financial strategy can be a transformative and empowering choice. So, seize the moment and explore how NFTs can unlock the magic of digital wealth in your life.

Epilogue

As we conclude our exhilarating journey through the world of Non-Fungible Tokens (NFTs) in "Unlocking the Potent Magic of Wealth with NFTs," it is imperative to reflect on the transformative power of NFTs and their profound role in shaping the future of wealth. In this concluding chapter, we will delve even deeper into the possibilities that await in the NFT-driven world, shedding light on the evolving landscape, emerging trends, and the enduring legacy of this innovative technology.

1. **NFTs: A Digital Renaissance of Wealth Creation** NFTs have ushered in a digital renaissance, where traditional notions of wealth and ownership are evolving. With the unique properties of NFTs, individuals now can amass wealth through digital assets that are scarce, verifiable, and easily transferable. The past chapters have showcased how NFTs have disrupted various industries, from art and entertainment to gaming and real estate, paving the way for new avenues of wealth generation.

2. **NFTs as a Store of Value** In the world of cryptocurrencies, Bitcoin has long been heralded as digital gold, a store of value that transcends borders and traditional financial systems. NFTs, however, are emerging as a unique form of digital wealth, offering collectors and creators the opportunity to store and appreciate value in the digital realm. As NFT adoption continues to grow, these digital assets are becoming integral components of diversified portfolios.

3. **NFTs and Diversification** Diversification is a fundamental strategy for managing wealth, and NFTs are expanding the horizons of diversification. By investing in various NFT assets across different categories and platforms, individuals can spread their risk while enjoying the potential for substantial returns. It

is essential to keep a pulse on the NFT market's ebbs and flows, recognizing that diversification can mitigate risks associated with this nascent industry.

4. **NFTs: An Ecosystem of Opportunities** The NFT ecosystem is continuously evolving, presenting a dynamic landscape of opportunities. Whether you are an artist, collector, investor, or enthusiast, there is a niche within the NFT world that aligns with your interests and goals. Exploring these opportunities requires a keen understanding of the market dynamics, artistic trends, and technological developments.

5. **NFTs Beyond Art and Collectibles** While art and collectables have captured the limelight in the NFT space, it is essential to realize that NFTs extend far beyond these domains. The use cases for NFTs are diverse, spanning virtual real estate, in-game items, digital fashion, and intellectual property rights. As NFT technology matures, its applications will continue to diversify, making it a critical component of the future wealth landscape.

6. **NFT Communities: The Heart of Wealth Creation** NFT communities have played an instrumental role in fostering wealth creation within this ecosystem. These communities offer support, education, and networking opportunities. By participating actively, individuals can access exclusive drops, collaborations, and insights that can significantly impact their NFT portfolios.

7. **Legal and Ethical Considerations** The road to wealth through NFTs is not without obstacles. Legal and ethical concerns have emerged as critical considerations in the NFT space. Issues related to copyright, fraud, and environmental sustainability are being addressed through regulation and industry self-governance. Staying informed about these evolving legal and ethical dimensions is paramount for responsible wealth creation.

8. **NFTs and the Decentralized Future** The promise of decentralization is at the core of blockchain technology, and NFTs are no exception. NFTs empower individuals to own and transact without intermediaries, aligning with the decentralized ethos of the blockchain. This shift towards decentralized finance (DeFi) and governance in the NFT space underscores the potential for innovative financial solutions and wealth creation mechanisms.

9. **NFTs in Everyday Life** NFTs are no longer confined to the digital art world or exclusive online platforms. They are permeating everyday life, from virtual real estate purchases to digital fashion statements. Integrating NFTs into everyday life is a testament to their mainstream acceptance and the opportunities they present for the average individual to grow their wealth.

10. **NFTs and Financial Inclusion** Wealth creation is not a privilege solely for the elite; it should be accessible to all. NFTs, with their fractional ownership and low entry barriers, offer an avenue for financial inclusion. This chapter delves into how NFTs can help bridge the wealth gap, providing opportunities for those who were previously excluded from traditional financial systems.

11. **Sustainability and NFTs** The environmental impact of NFTs has been a topic of concern, given the energy consumption of blockchain networks. This chapter explores sustainable practices and the emerging solutions that aim to reduce the carbon footprint of NFTs, ensuring that wealth creation is not at the expense of the planet.

12. **Emerging Trends** The NFT landscape is ever-evolving, and it's crucial to stay ahead of the curve. Emerging trends, such as the integration of NFTs in the metaverse, virtual reality experiences, and the fusion of physical and digital assets, are

shaping the future of wealth creation. Exploring these trends can provide a strategic advantage to NFT enthusiasts.

13. **NFTs and Cultural Impact** Beyond the financial realm, NFTs are leaving an indelible mark on culture and society. This chapter delves into how NFTs are redefining notions of ownership, creativity, and collaboration. The cultural impact of NFTs is integral to their role in shaping the future of wealth, as it drives demand and innovation.

14. **Education and NFT Mastery** To navigate the complex world of NFTs effectively, one must invest in education. This chapter emphasizes the importance of continuous learning and mastery, whether you are an artist, collector, or investor. NFT education can be the key to informed decisions and successful wealth creation.

15. **Conclusion: The Wealth of Possibilities** In conclusion, the world of NFTs is an enchanting realm of wealth creation that is still unfolding. As you close this book, we leave you with the realization that NFTs are not merely an investment vehicle or a passing trend; they represent a wealth of possibilities for individuals willing to explore, adapt, and innovate. The transformative power of NFTs is undeniable, and their role in shaping the future of wealth is nothing short of revolutionary.

Final Words

In this groundbreaking book, **"Unlocking the Potent Magic of Wealth with NFTs,"** we embark on a captivating journey through the transformative landscape of Non-Fungible Tokens (NFTs). These digital assets, which have revolutionized the concept of ownership and value in the virtual realm, have garnered unprecedented attention and investment in recent years. From their modest beginnings as a novel concept within the blockchain community to their pervasive influence across diverse industries, NFTs have emerged as a powerful tool for wealth creation and innovation.

The genesis of the NFT phenomenon can be traced back to the early 2010s when the concept of unique digital assets began to take shape within the burgeoning blockchain ecosystem. However, it was not until the mid-2010s that NFTs gained substantial traction, primarily within the realm of digital art and collectables. Artists and creators quickly recognized the potential of NFTs to authenticate and monetize their digital works, providing them with an avenue to reach a global audience while retaining control over their creations.

The impact of NFTs extends far beyond the art world, permeating various sectors, including entertainment, gaming, real estate, and even traditional finance. One of the most notable facets of NFTs lies in their ability to imbue digital assets with a sense of rarity and exclusivity, thereby enhancing their intrinsic value. This unique characteristic has led to a paradigm shift in the way we perceive and trade digital assets, unlocking new avenues for wealth accumulation and financial empowerment.

In the realm of art, NFTs have empowered artists to transcend the limitations of traditional galleries and auction houses, allowing them to directly connect with a global audience of collectors and enthusiasts. The ability to tokenize and sell digital art as NFTs has democratized the art market, enabling artists of all backgrounds to gain recognition and financial success. Notable platforms such as Foundation, SuperRare, and Rarible have provided artists with a decentralized marketplace to showcase their works and interact with a burgeoning community of art connoisseurs and investors.

Beyond the realm of art, NFTs have permeated the entertainment industry, providing content creators with innovative avenues to engage their audiences and monetize their intellectual property. Musicians, filmmakers, and content producers have leveraged NFTs to offer exclusive access to limited-edition content, merchandise, and immersive experiences, thereby fostering a deeper connection with their fan base and augmenting their revenue streams.

Similarly, the gaming industry has experienced a paradigm shift with the integration of NFTs, as virtual assets and in-game items can now be tokenized, traded, and owned securely on the blockchain. Players can acquire rare and unique in-game assets, such as skins, weapons, and collectables, which hold tangible value within and beyond the confines of the gaming universe. This convergence of gaming and blockchain technology has ushered in a new era of digital ownership and monetization, providing gamers with a tangible stake in the virtual worlds they inhabit.

Moreover, the integration of NFTs within the real estate sector has redefined the traditional property ownership model, offering investors and homeowners a transparent and secure platform to trade and fractionalize real estate assets. Through the tokenization of properties, individuals can invest in high-value real estate projects and diversify their portfolios, thereby gaining access to previously inaccessible avenues of wealth generation and passive income.

However, the allure of NFTs as a vehicle for wealth creation is not without its complexities and challenges. The volatility of the NFT market, coupled with concerns surrounding the environmental impact of blockchain technology, has spurred a discourse on the ethical implications of NFT ownership and trading. Additionally, the proliferation of counterfeit and fraudulent NFTs has underscored the importance of robust security measures and due diligence within the NFT ecosystem, emphasizing the need for comprehensive regulations and industry standards to safeguard the interests of creators and investors alike.

Navigating the intricacies of the NFT landscape requires a nuanced understanding of the underlying blockchain technology and the mechanics of tokenization. Investors and creators must acquaint themselves with the fundamental concepts of smart contracts, decentralized finance (DeFi), and the interoperability of blockchain networks to leverage the full potential of NFTs as a vehicle for wealth creation and asset diversification.

As we gaze into the horizon of the digital frontier, the future of NFTs appears promising and rife with possibilities. The convergence of art, technology, and finance within the NFT ecosystem has laid the groundwork for a new era of creative expression, financial inclusion, and digital ownership. Whether you are an aspiring artist seeking to showcase your talent, an investor looking to diversify your portfolio, or simply an enthusiast curious about the intersection of technology and finance, "Unlocking the Potent Magic of Wealth with NFTs" serves as your compass, guiding you through the intricacies and opportunities presented by this transformative digital phenomenon.

Dive into the pages of this book and immerse yourself in the captivating world of NFTs, where creativity meets commerce, and the power of wealth creation knows no bounds. As you embark on this enlightening journey, may you unlock the potent magic of NFTs and chart a course towards a prosperous and digitally empowered future.

Author Page
Nabal Kishore Pande

I was born on the 3rd of July in 1968, in the serene village of Kunalta, nestled in the picturesque Pithoragarh District of Uttarakhand, India. My parents, Mrs. Urmila Pandey and Mr. Prakash Chandra Pandey provided me with a nurturing environment that shaped my life's journey.

In 2003, I found the love of my life in Bhagwati Pandey, and together we welcomed our beloved daughter, Mahak Pandey, into the world in 2005. Currently, my family and I call 39 SSB Gate, Sinalpata Aincoli, Pithoragarh, Uttarakhand, our home.

Contact Information:

You can reach out to me through various means:

Mobile: +91-9557967893

LinkedIn: https://t.co/VBWr8vqjAV

Email: ernawal67@gmail.com

Twitter: @ernawal67

Telegram: @ernawal

Blogger: ernawal.blogspot.com

Facebook: https://t.co/lXefpSJBSe

My Background:

I am a dynamic professional with a background in Electrical Engineering and management. Over the years, I've cultivated a unique blend of skills, encompassing effective communication, project management, and industrial planning. But my professional journey is just one facet of my life.

My Literary Journey:

Beyond my professional pursuits, I've ventured into the realm of writing, becoming an author and a blogger. Through my writing, I explore a wide range of subjects, driven by my insatiable curiosity and love for storytelling.

My Published Works:

My literary journey has led to the publication of numerous books, each delving into diverse subjects and genres. Some of my published works include:

- Time-Tasted Test
- Lethal Illusion
- Taste of Bihar
- Shared Futures (21st Century Indo-US Odyssey)

- Romantic Reverie
- Wonders Unveiled
- Spectral Chronicles
- The Churning Seas
- Health and Beauty (Nurturing the Inner Glow)
- Sunny and Magical Forests Adventures
- Chronicles of Five Tales
- Post by Ghost
- Uttarakhand Trails and Tales
- Nature's Abode

Languages:

I take pride in being a multilingual author and communicator, allowing me to connect with readers from diverse backgrounds. My language skills include:

- **Hindi:** My native language
- **English:** Proficient in British English
- **Kumouni:** My native dialect of Hindi, reflecting my deep roots in the region of Uttarakhand, India.

My Story:

My journey began in the idyllic village of Kunalta, surrounded by the natural beauty and cultural richness of remote Uttarakhand. As I pursued my education, I excelled in Electrical Engineering and management, developing a unique blend of technical expertise and management acumen.

Throughout my career, I've been passionate about effective communication, project management, and industrial planning. These skills, combined with my love for storytelling, led me to explore various genres of writing.

My books cover a wide array of subjects, from the intricacies of culinary experiences to thought-provoking explorations of shared futures between nations. I've also ventured into the realms of romantic fiction, speculative fiction, and even health and beauty, nurturing the inner glow of my readers.

Connecting with Me:

In addition to my books, I maintain an active online presence. My blog, "**ernawal.blogspot.com**," provides a platform for sharing my thoughts and insights on a myriad of subjects. You can also find me on social media platforms like Twitter and LinkedIn, where I engage with readers and fellow authors.

My writing is deeply connected to my roots in Uttarakhand, India, and driven by a passion for exploring diverse subjects. Whether through my fiction or non-fiction works, I strive to create a personal connection that resonates with readers from all walks of life.

Milton Keynes UK
Ingram Content Group UK Ltd.
UKHW020645041223
433752UK00018B/1202

9 798223 856849